Imagination and Reflection:

A CHILD'S POETRY

MOHAMMAD
IBRAHEEM SHEIKH

INDIA · SINGAPORE · MALAYSIA

ISBN
Paperback 979-8-89588-308-2
Hardcase 979-8-89588-651-9

Contents

Preface

Welcome to my first poetry collection. As a young author, I'm excited to share this journey with you, filled with imagination, emotions and moments that have shaped my understanding of the nature around me.

Each poem in this book is a glimpse into my soul, capturing my feelings, observations and thoughts. From childhood experiences to the beauty of nature, these verses represent my effort to understand the world around me.

As you read, I hope you find echoes of your own experiences and pieces of your own story woven into mine. Poetry has a unique power of transcending our individual experiences, bringing us together and bridging the gaps between our unique journeys.

To my fellow young writers: continue writing. Your voice matters, and your stories deserve an audience. This book marks the beginning of my journey, and I'm eager to see where your words will lead you.

Thank you for joining me on this adventure. As you flip through the pages, I hope these poems inspire and uplift you, encouraging you to explore the magic of your own words.

With love,
Mohammad Ibraheem Sheikh

Captured by Mohammad Ibraheem Sheikh

Captured by Mohammad Ibraheem Sheikh

Acknowledgement

First, I would like to express my heartfelt gratitude to Almighty God for illuminating my path and guiding me through the entire writing journey of this book. He bestowed me with creativity and strength to express my thoughts and emotions through joyful verses.

I sincerely wish to express my profound thanks to my parents for encouraging my imagination and believing in me. Your unwavering support has nurtured my growth and enhanced my writing skills. I am incredibly thankful for all that you have done for me. Likewise, I would also like to extend my sincere appreciation to all my extended family, including my caring grandparents and wonderful cousins. Your influence in my life means the world, and I truly cherish every one of you.

I would also like to thank all my teachers and mentors at Al Falah International Delhi Public School, Jeddah. You taught me the magic of words and power of expression, inspiring me to begin writing on a variety of topics.

A special thanks to my school friends for listening to my written work on multiple occasions encouraging my growth as an author. Your smiles and laughter give me the courage to share my work.

Finally, to all the readers, I feel compelled to thank you from the bottom of my heart for dedicating your time to read my poems. I hope my blissful verses resonate with you, ignite your imagination, and bring you happiness.

The Good Old Days

The rooster has given its call
The dew drops now stop to fall

Will those days ever come back?
When your school bag used to look like a sack

The good old days
Surely had better rays

The dawn leisurely starts to fold
More like a rock revealing gold

The birds would sing so gracefully on the trees
And the hives would get busy with deafening bees

The peasants would collect their hoes to plough
their fields
For the living from the wheat that yields

Those days were like a six on a dice
It passed very pleasantly and nice

The Rose

In fields of green, I seek a rose
Red and pretty with the elegance it shows

Half underground, half on land
Produces beauty just like a sweat gland

Touch a petal it will soothe your finger
The breeze calmly hums and it looks like the rose
is a singer

Varying in all colors from white, red and pink
It is a very pleasing moment, you can't
afford to blink

Be careful if you are next to one which is fully
grown
If you make a mistake, blood is dripping due
to a thorn

Wither and bloom, wither and bloom
Always bright and fair, even in the state of gloom

The Woods

As the sun rises once again
A striking place comes in eyes
Every home is here from nests to a den
Every animal is here from birds to flies

Each leaf on a branch has its own story to tell
Each bark of a tree has its own identity to show
Every leaf has an adventure from its birth till it
has fell
Every seed is important for all have to grow

Every sound is heard here, from squeaks to a roar
Each one deserves respect and glory
Each species lives here galore
Each one here live together in harmony

The Morning

When the light crosses a long path
Each star in the sky hides
For the sky has stopped its dew bath
And the sun starts to rise from the east sides

Each soul opens its own eyes
And the moon conceals its appearance from every
one's view
The amount of light gently rise
How the night flew so fast still no one knew

The flowers once again bloom while the trees dance
And the houses become live
To capture the sun rise, you only have one chance
Everyone is glad from cities to beehive

The Breath in a Village

When the sun reveals its light
A rooster shares a well-known voice
Slowly the farmers in the fields come in sight
And the village starts to fill with noise

The cows leave for the meadow
And the birds seek their fare
The oxen load the seeds they always sow
While the blue sky shows the sun's dazzling glare

The flowers find attention
And birds perform their song
The children arrive at school for their education
I have been waiting for this beautiful moment since
very long

The Garden

When a seed begins its life
And a flower begins its blooming season
Each blade in a grass becomes as sharp as knife
And the birds come here for a reason

The tall trees show their height
And the delight is found in every bed
From lilies to daisies, every flower is in sight
Strawberry to carrot every plant is spread

The lamps and fences lay there too
Grass, beds and plants is a huge burden
Water and plant here is what most people do
From humans to animals every loves a garden

When I board a rocket for a ride
It goes off into the sky
What a view you find from each side
What a pleasure to see it so high

Slowly, I see mercury's mass
Venus and earth look like twins
Then a red planet appears, which used to have earth's grass
What a sight! From Jupiter's dot to Saturn's amusing spins

Then I watch the stunning space rocks
And the belt after Jupiter in a race
The rivers on earth look like tiny blocks
What an adventurous day in space

The Sheep

Oh sheep always grazing the field
Eating as fast as you could
You really look like a winter shield
Helping man as much as you would

Always running from humans because of fear
It is because you don't want to be cooked as meat
You get terrified from sheep cries when you hear
Black as they are your big feet

Your wool has many people after it
All you want is fresh green grass
Sadly, in the plates you sometimes fit
Doesn't really matter small or big which one is
your mass

 A Tree

In a park so large, I notice a tree
Fruits and leaves, that is all you see

Birds chirp so high in the sky
Watch and write on the ground I lie

A trunk I see so hollow and grey
Hard and rough what can I say

Sometimes small, sometimes huge
I wonder, what is your secret in your beauty that
you fuse

Every spring, I see a flower so attractive
My friend tree, without you how can we live

A Park

A park where trees stand high and tall
Some people rest in shades
Children and friends have fun playing ball
And the little girls tie their braids

The branches sway here and there
And the colors gleam bright
To find sadness here is very rare
While the sun fills the earth with light

The benches and tables stand on the green grounds
Some people rest against a tree's bark
If you sit carefully, you can notice bugs and their
sounds
You would love to visit such a park

Spring

When the flowers bloom, and the trees bear fruits
The sunshine fills the earth with light
The birds migrate through long routes
And the sky becomes clear and bright

Some people travel from seas or a bay
And the streams in the plains naturally run
Kids are enjoying their holiday
Looks like everyone is having fun

A Pretty Daisy

In fields where grass and plants grow
A daisy stands on its stalk
The daisies get big and big but never show
Amazes people when they walk

Consist of two colors, yellow and white
In a shape made like a cross
Each petal assembled very beautifully and light
Loosing even a single flower in the world is a big
loss

When they spread from fields to homes
Everyone gets lost in their imagination
They come with springs and each one blooms
May God keep them on earth from generation to
generation

A Day at the Amusement Park

When I enter an amusement park
I see many rides, scary and fun
Some in the day and other in the dark
Delight filled in each one

When rollercoasters loop and Ferris wheels turn
Screams and laughter fill within the air
Try each ride that is what most people learn
Others have a popcorn treat and relax on a chair

Soon the Merry-go-rounds begin
While the toys drag attention
The cotton candy machine starts to spin
Every day, people here have a celebration

The Ocean

When the light falls on the surface of the crust
A common place reveals itself
The breeze and wind blow away the dust
While the fish seek their fare them self

Some fish swim here and there in shoals
And the seaweeds sway left to right
The predators and sharks keep some rules
Keep an eye out so jellyfish don't bite

Each specie swim here from salmons to whales
And each one behave in their own way
Don't freak out if you see a thresher shark's tail
An ocean surrounds everything from an island
to a bay

A Day at the Zoo

When a lion roars and a bird sings
Each person here gets filled with joy
From the entrance, everyone's excitement starts to
swing
Each girl and boy happily enjoy

First we see the tall giraffe
On a towering height with a huge appetite
Performing its graceful laugh
And the lion roaring with all its might

Then we look at the elephant's huge mass
And the monkey's playful behavior in a troop
We hear the brays of donkey and ass
And the flamingoes in the water in a group

At last when we buy a treat or two
Each man or women's brain gets stuffed with
memories
When you go in the car, you look at the sky clear
and blue
Wondering that when you will visit again such
glories

When the Night Falls

When the last ray of sun falls on earth
Everyone goes back to their home
And a new beginning takes birth
Each person's eyes reflect gloom

Each bird flies back to its nest
And cow's return from the fields and meadows
Farmers too comeback after trying their best
And rays drag away the shadows

The sun throws rays behind mountains
And the light is no longer in sight
The water keeps gushing out from natural
fountains
And every one watches the night

A Ride on a Roller Coaster

When the seats get free and it is time to board
Every seat in the ride gets quickly sat on
For each person wants to explore the scary road
Up and up there it is gone

High and far there it goes
Everyone gets ready for their laugh and screams
And when it loops, everyone cries from the pain of
their toes
Each kid thinking, are they in dreams

When it finally starts to descend
Everyone's heart is filled with relief
New people are now sent
Exploring is fun with people of different belief

A Day at the Beach

When the waves and tides collide with the shore
A child builds his own sea castle
The wind and breeze fiercely roar
And a man enjoys eating his apple

Teens enjoy to play volleyball
And the kids gently fly their kites
The adults watch the view from high walls
And sun fills the sand with various lights

At sunset when the sun hides behind the sea
And it attracts attention of everyone
I would like to visit such a beach if you ask me
Where I would experience all day fun

Colors of the Sky

When the morning sun rises
The sky shows its color blue
Fluffy clouds float in the air of various sizes
And the grass absorbs the dew

As the noon reaches its time
The sun shows its warm ray
Of today's experience, this is just a dime
The same thing happens every day

As the dusk paints the sky orange and pink
A light along with the rays fly
Each gleaming light hide and sink
And different lights make the colors of the sky

A Day with the Birds

When a pigeon takes its flight
And the sparrows sing to wake up each one
You see falcons in the sky, what a sight!
While in Africa Ostriches love to run

Then the parrots talk
And the flycatchers fetch their meals
And the emus quickly walk
To have a pet Macaw would be one of the best deals

At last we have the colorful peacock
And the vultures roaming through the sky
While the Cassowary is strong enough to lift a rock
What a fine day with the birds to fly

When the Rain Falls

When the clouds burst, a water drop falls
It lands on the earth with a long tale
Leaving traces and signs on the walls
As if the skies were to send us a message in a mail

Each drop dances on the floor
With its own rhythm to show
Cooling down the crust and core
A gleaming light in each one that loves to glow

When it goes inside the earth very deep
It waters the plants very fast
It shows itself in heaps and heap
Each drop is important from first to last

Biography

Mohammad Ibraheem Sheikh, author of "Imagination and Reflection: A Child's Poetry", was born on 16th September 2013 in the picturesque, serene valley of Kashmir, India, but, raised in the vibrant coastal city of Jeddah, Saudi Arabia, where his father is a University Professor. This young author has a unique perspective shaped by two diverse cultures. He was always mesmerized by the beautiful landscapes of his native place and the unique city of Jeddah where the Arabian desert meets the tranquil waters of the Red Sea. He is a fifth-grade student at Al Falah International Delhi Public School, Jeddah, fuelled by a deep passion for writing. Beyond his love for writing, Ibraheem has immense zeal for painting, and is an ardent soccer player dedicating considerable time to football. He also possesses a deep understanding and exceptional skill in roller skating, and has earned Black belt in Taekwondo at a very young age. Alongside his sports activities, his writing journey started at the age of six when his parents, particularly his mother introduced him to the world of children's story books and rhymes. The colorful evocative depiction and the joyful language stimulated his imagination, catalyzing his creative expression. As a result, he soon began to compose his own stories and poetry, and achieved his dream of publishing first poetry collection in 2024. The book features a variety of delightful poems that evoke nature and childhood experiences, appealing to both children and adults alike.